Economic Fallacies Exposed

Geoffrey Wood

City University Business School

Published by The Institute of Economic Affairs
1997

First published in October 1997 by
The Institute of Economic Affairs
2 Lord North Street
Westminster
London SW1P 3LB

Occasional Paper 102
All rights reserved
ISSN 0073-909X
ISBN 0-255 36407-5

Printed in Great Britain by
Hartington Fine Arts Limited, Lancing, West Sussex
Set in Times Roman 11 on 13 point

Contents

[3]

[4]

Part 1
Regulation and Markets

'Ticket Touts Are Harmful and Wicked. They Should Be Stamped Out by Law.'

THERE IS AN IDEA about that being a ticket tout is in some unexplained way disreputable, and that those who deal with them, whether buying or selling, are disgracing themselves and their associates. One cannot refute a moral judgement by logic. It is not a matter of economics. But what economics *can* do is to show that ticket touts are useful, and that they provide a service to both seller and buyer. There is absolutely no case for making their activities illegal.

To see this, think about what a ticket tout does. And just for the moment, we shall not call what he trades in 'tickets' – we shall call them 'the item'.

Some person has a supply of the item surplus to what he wants. The item does not keep for ever – indeed, after a certain date it becomes useless. He can do several things with it – give it away, not use it (and thus let it go to waste), or he can sell it. If he wants to sell it, there are many methods open to him; but a very convenient one is to find someone who deals in the item, and is willing to buy it with the aim of reselling it, but bearing the risk that he may fail. The original possessor of the item, who is not a professional dealer, is willing to sell for a little less than he might receive from the final consumer in return for someone else bearing the risk of not selling the item.

The intermediary now has a stock of them, which he tries to sell. He tries to sell at a price higher than he paid, to people who want to buy it.

Now consider the whole transaction. One person had some items surplus to his wants. He sells them to someone who then tries to sell them to a person who does want to use them. No-one has been harmed by the chain of transactions – and that is fortunate, for there are millions of such transactions every day. A newsagent buys newspapers and sells them on. A grocer buys food and sells it on. A dealer in government securities buys them and sells them on. We don't attach the discreditable name of 'tout' to newsagents, grocers, and bond dealers and say their activities should be made illegal. Why do we do it to dealers in tickets?

[13]

If we ban ticket touts, we would be making both buyers and sellers worse off. And by making illegal a harmless activity which benefits all who take part in it, it would divert police effort away from dealing with real crime. The idea that ticket touts should be banned is nonsense.

June 1989

The Conduct of an Industry – in Particular, How it Serves Consumers – Is Improved by Government Regulation

IT IS WIDELY BELIEVED that government intervention in industry can and does benefit consumers. Economists have developed careful and clear analyses of the situations when regulation could be desirable. But does regulation in practice have these desirable effects?

Adam Smith certainly doubted its efficiency. To restrain people from entering into voluntary transactions 'is a manifest violation of that natural liberty which it is the proper business of law not to infringe but to support'. Nevertheless, he argued, 'those exertions of the natural liberty of a few individuals which might endanger the security of the whole society, are, and ought to be, restrained by the laws of all governments...' He defended regulation in such cases in principle. But he objected to the practice. The legislature, he argued, is directed not by a view of the common good, but 'the clamorous importunity of special interests'. His view was that whatever regulation could do in theory, in practice it usually benefits those regulated.

What does the evidence say? A pioneer in this area is George Stigler. In a study of the electricity industry in the US, he found that regulation affected neither rates charged to customers nor profits earned for shareholders. In a study of the securities industry, he found that regulation governing the listing of new securities, presumably intended to protect the investor, had no significant effect on the returns to new shares as compared to ones already in the market.

A current UK example which should lead one to wonder about the benefits of regulation is food. When it was feared that eggs were likely to be harmful, and sales dropped, egg farmers were offered compensation – which was paid of course by a levy on consumers, who had just very plainly indicated in the market that they did not wish to support egg farmers! In contrast, how was a different group, one not close or important to the regulators, treated? Producers of non-pasteurised cheeses – a tiny group of farmers – and foreign cheese makers, were both threatened with

[15]

having their products banned on health grounds before consumers had a chance to show if they were concerned!

Regulation has two vices. It restricts competition – all producers are compelled to behave in a similar way. And it restricts information – information has to go to the regulator, but not to the consumers who buy the product. Informed choice is not possible without information; and restricting competition means that there is less pressure to raise quality and lower cost. For these reasons, regulation by government generally harms the consumer. The best regulation is by competition combined with provision of information.

August 1989

The State Should Step In to Protect the Environment

THERE IS NOW WIDESPREAD popular concern about the 'quality of life' and the environment. Both are said to be deteriorating and, it is claimed, this can be stopped only by the state preventing destructive private actions which have no regard for the consequences for people. We need, it is said, planning to protect the world.

This is in many cases the opposite of the truth. It is state action that is the destroyer, private the preserver.

Two examples are useful. Consider the rail link to the Channel Tunnel. Even in its revised form this will be destructive – of how people want to live or visit. That is not a private action. It is the result of the state giving a body – British Rail – the right to dispossess people of something at a price below that which would induce them to move voluntarily.

Town planning is another example. Buildings can be put up when permission is given – regardless of the wishes of those who live nearby – at the whim of a civil servant or the vote-catching urge of a politician.

Both these problems arise because politicians either take away property rights or refuse to acknowledge their existence. If people have rights in property – if they own it – they will preserve it.

Consider the above two examples. If people had to be paid to leave their homes or tolerate a train near their garden, the costs to society of building the rail link would be taken into account. If owners of houses were entitled to compensation for a hideous new building increasing congestion around them, again the cost of the building would be taken into full account.

This would produce efficient resource allocation; costs would be taken fully into account. And it would also produce the desired amount of preservation. Not, no doubt, everyone's desired amount – too much for some, too little for others. But it would produce what people were willing to pay for.

Acknowledging property rights in the environment would thus serve two purposes. More efficient resource allocation would take place. And the present debate about preserving the environment would be clarified. At the moment people call for preservation unthinkingly because the costs do not fall on them. If the cost of resisting a development was not being paid a large sum in compensation, then the objectors would think. As it is, they might as well resist.

Acknowledging property rights in the environment would preserve what people want. Not acknowledging these rights, having state planning, leaves the present and future environment up to the accidents of election timing and chance.

December 1989

Part 2
International Trade and Finance

One Country Should Not Cut Its Tariffs Unless Others Do

A COMMON CLAIM is that tariff reduction, perhaps even to the extent of moving to completely free trade, has to be reciprocal. One country it is said should not on its own adopt free trade. Some proponents of this recognise that unilateral free trade is beneficial, but use the promise of tariff reduction as a bargaining device to get other countries to reduce their tariffs. Some people claim that unilateral free trade is harmful. That is a fallacy, and one which can be very damaging.

If a country has no tariff barriers (or other barriers to international trade) it benefits in two ways. It benefits in consumption and it benefits in production.

The consumption benefits are the most obvious. Consumers can buy what they want wherever it is produced most cheaply, whether it is at home or abroad. There are not tariffs to make home produced goods artificially cheap compared to those produced overseas; or, perhaps, to divert demand from the cheapest foreign supplier to one who, although more expensive, has from political favour won a lower tariff against his goods.

Consumers, in summary, can make the most of their income if they live in a country with no impediments to international trade. But of course consumers either are or depend on producers – to get the income they consume. Could free trade not harm producers? The answer is that it could – and probably would harm some. But the economy as a whole would still gain. The reason is as follows. Producers are guided by the prices they see confronting them to produce what is most profitable for them and to do so as cheaply as they can. Prices thus direct resources to where they are most useful, as those producers to whom they are most valuable will pay most for them. If an economy is trading freely, without tariffs, its resources are making the most of the opportunities prescribed to them by the pattern of prices in the rest of the world.

The economy's resources will thus be used where it is most productive, relative to the rest of the world, for them to be. The economy will be making the most of the opportunities available to it. (These opportunities would of course be greater if all the world were a free trade area, but that is not really something any one country can produce.)

It is possible to construct a theoretical example where a country gains benefit by imposing tariffs, as these shift prices in its favour. But this example depends on the implausible assumption of great monopoly power and other countries not objecting and retaliating.

In summary, free trade is the best course a country can follow. Any other course impoverishes the country – by making production inefficient and denying consumers access to the cheapest markets. Protection is totally unjustifiable.

November 1991

Foreign Exchange Speculation
Should Be Stopped

ATTACKS ON FOREIGN EXCHANGE speculators have recently come from, among many others, the US Treasury Secretary and the Labour Party's Shadow Chancellor. It might be thought that there must be something in a view that unites such diverse political standpoints. Not so. All the unanimity shows is the ability of politicians to be wrong together – to display the herdlike mentality of which they accuse speculators.

What is speculation? In the foreign exchanges it is selling a currency in the expectation that its value will fall, or buying it expecting its value to rise. Speculation of course can occur in any market – it is just trading in the expectation of making a profit from future price changes. Who does it? Banks, acting on their own account, and also acting for clients. Their clients can include insurance companies, pension funds and all sorts of commercial firms.

What exactly is wrong with this activity? Note first that if speculators are wrong in their expectation they lose money. For if, to give an example, they buy a currency expecting its price to rise, and it does not, then they lose at the very least their transaction costs. So *mistaken* speculation – speculation whose expectations are falsified – is unlikely to be a persistent problem.

If speculators tend on average to move exchange rates to a 'correct' level, why do governments object to them? The answer lies in the meaning of the word 'correct'. They may well be exchange rates which governments do not like – but exchange rates which are nevertheless the consequence of government policies. Governments often wish to achieve an end, but are unwilling to conduct policy accordingly. In other words, governments dislike speculators because speculators expose the weaknesses or the incompetence of governments. Speculators do not 'attack' currencies for fun, on a whim. Most of the time the attack is mounted because politicians' actions are inconsistent with what they say they are trying to do.

By thus exposing governments, speculators not only make money for themselves; they are useful to society. Their actions should be welcomed.

November 1992

Free Trade Should Be Fair

VISITING THE UNITED STATES, one is struck by a particular aspect of the discussions of free international trade. The USA is moving towards a North American Free Trade Agreement (NAFTA) which aims, in principle, to remove all government-created trade barriers to the movement of goods between the countries of that area – Canada, the USA, and Mexico. But a major hindrance has emerged – environmental standards in Mexico.

It is not clear whether those who raise this difficulty are concerned about the environment, or concerned just to maintain protectionism. For now, let us give them the benefit of the doubt. Let us assume that they really believe that efficient international trade requires the same environmental standards of every country which engages in it. That fallacy is the one exposed in this column.

Why do countries engage in international trade? One obvious reason residents of one country buy goods from residents of another is that they cannot be produced at home. By far the greatest part of international trade is trade which takes place because some goods can be produced better or more cheaply (or both) in one country rather than in another.

What produces these price differences? (I focus on price differences henceforth as they are what is at issue.) Climate is one factor. Another, very important, is relative abundance of resources, making some cheaper in one country than in another. Note that it is relative abundance in two senses – in one country as compared to another, and abundance produced by ample supply *relative to demand*. For prices to be low, there needs to be an abundant supply of a good relative to the demand for it. There being a lot of the good, or a little, in the physical sense does not give any information about price.

Now to NAFTA and environmental standards, where the above discussion will help clarify matters and expose the fallacy. Mexico can produce some goods more cheaply than the USA for a variety of reasons. Among these reasons, and particularly important for some heavy industries, is that manufacturers in Mexico do not have to meet the same low pollution standards. Their 'smoke-stack industries' still have smoke stacks!

Why is this, and what would be the consequences of insisting that it be stopped before Mexico was allowed to export to the USA without any restrictions?

There are many reasons. Tastes vary. Smoke may be seen not as damaging to health, but as a symbol of thriving and prosperous industry. But one factor is almost certainly income. Lack of food and of clean water kills more rapidly than does a smoky atmosphere. People will buy food and clean water before worrying about clean air.

Suppose they were compelled to worry, and to do something about it. What would happen? Immediately, costs of production in Mexico would rise. Goods would be more expensive than before, and would either not be exported to the US or exported only in modest quantities, even if trade were free of impediments.

Well-being would be affected both in the US and in Mexico. US residents would not get some goods so cheaply and so would be worse off. Because they could not get these goods so cheaply, they could not afford to buy some other goods. The producers of such goods would be worse off, perhaps out of work. Meanwhile, some Mexicans would see the demand for their products disappear, and so they in turn could be unable to buy other goods, either from Mexico or elsewhere. In summary, both producers and consumers, in the USA and Mexico, would be made worse off if the Mexicans were not allowed to make use of some of their relatively abundant resources – cheap air, water and land. The policy makes no more sense than it would to say that, before the US is allowed to sell grain to Europe, it has to destroy the prairies.

What of the Mexican environment? Free trade between the US and Mexico will increase demand for all relatively cheap Mexican resources. Wages in Mexico will rise. And so will the value people put on clean air!

It is possible that environmental pollution will not diminish in Mexico. That would follow if Mexican tastes really were very different from those in other countries that have developed and become rich. In that unlikely event, it would not be grounds for preventing free trade – or at any rate no better grounds than it would be to prevent free trade with a country because its citizens wore brown shoes to the office.

Insisting that free trade requires similar environmental standards between countries before trade starts is equivalent to saying that all

[26]

relative advantages should be extinguished by law before trade starts. Acting in accordance with that fallacy would be a recipe for poverty in all the prospective trading partners.

September 1993

A Current Account Deficit Is a Problem

MANY COMMENTATORS LAMENT that Britain is running a deficit in the current account of the balance of payments. Some worry particularly about our deficit in goods – what is called the visible balance. The second concern is always misplaced. The first is slightly more complicated. It is therefore better to deal with the simple matter first.

International trade is basically of two *types* – trade in goods and trade in services. Exports of either generate foreign earnings, so, from that point of view, it does not matter what is exported. Indeed, it is perfectly normal as countries develop for them to produce and trade in services. International trade in services has been in recent years the fastest-growing part of such trade.

Some people worry because manufactured goods have become a smaller part of our output. That is a separate concern. But it is worth remarking that the arguments and evidence do not support the claim that it is intrinsically better to produce manufactured goods rather than services.[1]

Given that the composition of exports does not matter, what about their total? Does it matter if we are exporting fewer goods and services than we are importing?

The best way to answer this question is to start with another. How are we paying for these goods and services? Some of them are paid for by our export earnings. Others are paid for in one of two ways – by running down our savings or by borrowing. Like an individual or a company, more can be spent than is earned, provided savings are reduced or borrowing increased. There are many circumstances where such action is perfectly sensible. There can be favourable investment opportunities, a temporary drop in income, or a chance to buy something more cheaply than usual. There is nothing wrong with borrowing; what matters is what it is for. If spending is wasteful, it is wasteful whether current income or borrowed funds are used.

---

[1] An excellent review of these arguments is contained in N. F. R. Crafts's 1993 Hobart Paper, *Can De-industrialisation Seriously Damage Your Wealth?*, Hobart Paper No. 120, London: Institute of Economic Affairs, January 1993.

The same is true for a country. If individual decisions by residents, whether firms or individuals, lead to a current account deficit, then a decision has been taken to spend more than income. If the funds being borrowed to finance that spending are used wisely, there is no problem. If they are not used wisely, then it is foolish spending, *not* the act of borrowing, that is the problem.

A striking example occurred in the United States. On average, that country ran a deficit on current account from the last quarter of the 19th century into the first decade of the 20th. It did so because there was a tremendous demand for funds to invest. Population, industry, and agriculture were all expanding westwards. The funds were lent from the residents of European countries, where the expected rate of return on investment was on average lower than in the United States. No one – at any rate, no one I know of – has claimed that the decline of the US set in with that foreign borrowing. It was used productively. The balance-of-payments deficit it engendered was in no way symptomatic of a problem.

Sometimes such deficits can be symptoms of problems (though not problems in themselves). For example, the symptom can be of 'excess demand'. Easy monetary policy may have over-stimulated demand, leading not just to rising prices, but also (as goods become harder to obtain or more expensive at home) to more purchases from abroad. If the exchange rate is floating, it will be driven down. And if it is pegged, there will be pressure to devalue.

Before summing up, one point remains. If a country is borrowing abroad, it is not necessarily increasing *net* overseas indebtedness. That may seem surprising – if a person borrows, his or her debts increase. But even in that case, if he or she has assets, they may be increasing in value more rapidly than the new debts. The same can be true of a country. The value of Britain's overseas assets has in recent years increased more rapidly than her overseas debts; increasing borrowing need not, and in this case did not, bring increased indebtedness.

Now to conclude. Overseas earnings are overseas earnings; it does not matter whether they come from sale of goods or sale of services. A current account deficit – more goods and services being bought from abroad than are sold here – is not itself a problem. It implies foreign borrowing. What matters is not the borrowing, but what has produced it and what it is being spent on.

[29]

Current account imbalances are symptoms – but they can be symptoms of sensible decisions or of folly.

November 1993

EMU Will Eliminate Turbulence in the ERM

THE TURBULENCE IN THE ERM earlier this year – when Spain and Portugal devalued and France, Belgium and Denmark raised interest rates to defend their currencies – has been cited by some as a reason for hastening on to EMU. The argument is simple, and runs as follows. These countries found their exchange rates were being 'attacked by speculators', forcing undesirable changes in policy which would not have occurred without the speculative attacks: had there been no national currencies, the speculators could not have caused these problems. Hence, the argument concludes, abolishing national currencies and moving to a European currency will end the phenomenon of sensible policies being 'blown off course' by speculators.

That seems perfectly straightforward, provided one grants a crucial assumption – that speculators go around 'attacking' currencies without reason. In general, they do not.

Speculation involves buying and selling in the expectation of a price change. If the price is expected to rise, speculators buy; if it is expected to fall, speculators sell. Now suppose the speculators' forecasts are wrong. Suppose they buy in expectation of a price rise, and the price, instead of rising, falls. They have lost money. If that happened often enough, they would give up and go out of business. And of course many speculators do lose money and go out of business. But on average, they get it right.

It is important to be clear about what is being said. We are not saying that most speculators are never wrong in their judgements. We are not even saying that there are a few speculators who are never wrong. What is being said is that the average speculator is right sufficiently often to make profits. If that were not so, speculation, whether in currencies, corn or works of art, would have vanished from the face of the earth.

There is here an important implication for the claim that the ERM's recent troubles are a reason for hastening on to EMU. Now and again there *may* be a concerted attack on a currency which is not justified by underlying economic conditions and policies (though it is hard to find examples of such events). In general, however, speculative attacks are well founded – they are based on a sensible expectation about the future – otherwise speculators as a body would lose money.

This leads to two possibilities. Either the recent ERM stresses were without foundation – in which case the accompanying policy changes can, as will be argued below, quickly be reversed. Or alternatively, there was good reason for what took place. Suppose the first, and less likely, was the case. Then the speculative pressures would quickly vanish, as the speculators run out of money, and any policy changes they induced can be undone.

What of the second? In this event, the policy changes were required to restore some prospect of economic stability in the economies affected. The fact that the countries whose currencies devalued had very high unemployment rates and burgeoning budget deficits, while those where interest rates rose had budgetary problems, increased political uncertainty, or both, suggests that the attacks were not irrational.

In practice, exchange rate pressures will rarely cause fundamental policy changes – although they may trigger them. If there had been no exchange rate, policies would have to change anyway, although the timing might have been different.

Further, suppose exchange rates vanished in a common European currency. Assets in the countries which changed policy could still have been sold. Interest rates on their debt, already high, would have risen still further. Taking away the exchange rate simply removes one channel of adjustment to imbalance in the economy, and forces the other adjustments to be the greater.

To sum up, the idea that removing the exchange rate would stop markets responding to divergences among economies is fundamentally flawed – for two reasons. *First*, speculative attacks are usually based on a sound judgement of economic conditions – so the policy changes they prompt will come anyway. *Second*, abolishing the exchange rate leaves plenty of other markets in which to speculate – and by removing one market, it forces bigger changes on others.

The argument that ERM turbulence strengthens the case for EMU is an example of an old, and very common, fallacy – that removing the messenger who brings the news eliminates the news itself.

September 1995

Free Trade Causes Unemployment

FREE TRADE HAS OFTEN been an unpopular policy. Various arguments have been advanced against it at various times in the past. The one that has resurfaced recently, in the last US presidential election and now in the Republican Primary Campaigns before this year's presidential election in the United States, is that free trade – particularly between developed and less developed countries – will cause unemployment in the developed countries. (Interestingly, in the less developed countries fears about the consequences of trade with developed countries are sometimes voiced; these are addressed in a subsequent 'Economic Fallacies Exposed' column.)

In fact, it is not true that free trade causes unemployment. It may, however, have an effect on wages; this possibility is taken up below.

There are various reasons for engaging in foreign trade. Most obviously, one can buy goods not capable of being produced domestically. This comprises, when one thinks about it, rather a small group. Minerals, for example, may not be available. But beyond such categories, a lot can be produced if one does not mind the cost. Take the example of Scotland. That country – and Dundee in particular – is the world's leading producer of marmalade. Oranges are a crucial ingredient for that. They could be grown in Scotland – in hothouses; but they are not, because of the cost.

Cost differences account for a large part of international trade. People in one country buy from another country or countries goods which *can* be produced domestically, but only at a cost so high as to offset any saving in expenditure on transport.

There is a still further reason for engaging in international trade.

Suppose that one country was less efficient than the rest of the world in producing *every* good. Less efficient in the sense that it required more units of everything used in production (that is, of every 'factor of production', to use the technical term) to produce every good in that country than it did elsewhere. Could that country engage in trade? Should it?

The answers are that it both could and should. It can do so by tending to specialise in the production of what it is least bad at.

The reason is that, before trade opens up between this country and the rest of the world, prices within the country will be related to costs of production there. Hence the pattern of relative prices – the price of one good compared to others – will reflect these costs. This will also be true in the rest of the world. Therefore (except in an unusual special case, when *relative* costs of production are the same worldwide) relative prices before trade will be different in different countries. Now, where does that lead?

Suppose trade now opens up between countries. What will happen? People will see that relative prices differ in different countries, and will make their purchases accordingly. They will buy where goods are *relatively* cheaper. There will thus be two-way trade, even although one country has higher costs of production than the other. (The exchange rate will move so as to compensate for these production costs.)

The point is important, so an example may be helpful. Suppose in one country production costs are such that before trade the price ratio of two goods is 3:1; and in the other country, the ratio is 3:2. Then when trade opens up, consumers in the first country will wish to buy the first good overseas; and in the second country, they will wish to buy the second good overseas. Thus both countries take advantage of relative price differences produced by different production costs.

Each country will tend to specialise in the good which it is relatively more efficient at producing. And consumers in each country will gain, from a fall in the relative price of a good. But what about jobs?

It has so far been seen that trade can take place for three reasons, and that every one of these reasons leads to gains – in the form of either a wider choice of goods or a lower cost of some goods – for consumers.

These gains are, however, produced by a changing pattern of production. Within each economy, demand switches away from one good and towards the other (or others). What does this do to employment? Plainly it requires workers to move. It does not, however, put them completely out of a job. They are not wanted in one job but they *are* wanted in another – the same force which reduces demand for them in one activity increases demand in another. *The reduction and the increase in demand are*

[34]

inseparable. Trade does cause workers to move – but it does not cause unemployment.

There are two qualifications to the above conclusion. *First*, unless workers can move instantaneously, neither requiring retraining nor having to look for work, there will be a *temporary* rise in unemployment. *Second*, if the workers cannot become qualified to work in the new jobs – whether through lack of ability or because there are barriers to acquiring the qualification (very long apprenticeships required by law, for example) – then they will, indeed, become unemployed. But aside from that particular case, free trade does not cause permanent unemployment. At worst, it causes a temporary rise in it.

Trade can certainly affect the pattern of earnings in one activity as compared to another, for it changes the pattern of demand for what produces these goods. Models can be constructed which give clear-cut predictions of the effect of trade on the distribution of income. But when the complexities of the world are introduced into the models, the predictions are not so clear-cut. Relative wages are changing all the time, and trade plays a part in producing these changes; but the size, and sometimes the direction, of the effect is seldom unambiguous.

Free trade does not cause unemployment. What it *does* do is change patterns of demand within economies. This leads to changed patterns of employment, and there can be transitional unemployment while adjustment to this new pattern is going on. Those who maintain that trade cause permanent unemployment, or that the temporary unemployment it causes should be resisted, are really saying that the pattern of demand for goods should never change. For it is these changes that require changes in the structure of output, and they require changes *regardless* of what has produced the change in the pattern of demand.

Trade is only one of the many factors that cause economic change. Abandoning free trade would not prevent economic change; it would only make people poorer, by restricting the access to where goods are cheaper than at home. It is a recipe for poverty, and not even for poverty at high levels of employment.

June 1996

The Country Should Be More Competitive

POLITICIANS ARE FREQUENTLY SAYING that the country should be 'more competitive'. 'Competitiveness Reports' are produced. The country is compared to its 'overseas competitors'. The idea somehow gets about that Britain – or whatever country is being discussed – should be so good at producing goods and services that we need buy nothing at all from the rest of the world, and can sell anything we want to it. But the whole idea is a nonsense – as David Ricardo showed over 150 years ago.

Countries can be rich or poor, efficient or inefficient, but they can always compete in world markets. They specialise according to what is known as *comparative advantage*. And 'comparative' is a key word. The following demonstration of the argument is essentially Ricardo's.

Start by imagining a country which is not open to the rest of the world. It does not engage at all in foreign trade. But there is a market system inside that country. There is internal trade, between producers and consumers inside the country. The next point to observe is that there cannot be trade without there being prices. Prices are inevitably *established* by trade. There cannot be one without the other. (That may at first glance seem an odd thing to say. After all, we are accustomed to going in to shops and finding the prices already there. But these prices are set by the shopkeeper in the expectation of some trade pattern. If demand turned out differently from expected, prices would soon be changed.)

To summarise so far then, our imaginary economy, cut off from the rest of the world, has a fully developed set of relative prices (the prices of goods relative to other goods). Now imagine that the barriers between this imaginary country and the rest of the world vanish, and the citizens of this economy discover that relative prices are different overseas. For example, suppose that the internal prices were such that if you reduced your wine consumption by one bottle per year, you could with the money buy a pound of cheese. But you discover that overseas, the cheese you could buy if you gave up consuming a bottle of wine was only half-a-pound in weight. Cheese, in other words, was more expensive relative to wine abroad than it was at home.

What happens next? Foreigners would observe that by coming to this country and supplying wine, they could get more cheese than they could at home. For a bottle of wine would buy them a pound, not a half-pound of cheese. And residents of this country would also gain; for prices would adjust to reflect the increased demand for cheese, and they would end up with more wine than before and, if they wished, no less cheese.

Now residents of both countries have gained, and there has been no mention of how 'competitive' either economy is. We could now assume that to produce either good, either wine or cheese, our imaginary country which we started with required twice, or three times, or however many times we wished, the amount of inputs per unit of output as did the rest of the world. That does not matter. It does not prevent the economy engaging in, and gaining from, international trade.

Trade between countries is not a competition in which there are winners and losers. It is a mutually beneficial activity, from which both sides gain. (There is one special case. If, when a country opens up to trade, it finds that relative prices abroad are the same as they are at home, then there is no possibility of fruitful exchange. But there are no losses either. In that special case the country neither gains nor loses from trade.)

So, then, the notion that countries 'compete' with one another in international trade is totally misconceived. And not only misconceived. It can cause harm, if it leads to policies which impede international trade. If, for example, we start protecting firms by tariffs or subsidies to produce 'national champions' then we are wasting resources.

Nevertheless, that said, it is necessary to be fair to those who talk of national 'competition'. Obviously, it is better to be more productive rather than less. For the more productive one is, the better off one is. Some at least of the schemes to make us more 'competitive' are actually designed to make us more productive. And that is unequivocally a good thing.

So, to sum up. First, the idea that nations 'compete' with one another in international trade is totally misguided. It can lead to harmful policies. Countries gain by engaging in trade with the rest of the world. Trade is a mutually beneficial activity, not a competition. If policies justified by 'competitiveness' are actually intended to raise productivity, then they are aimed at a sensible

[37]

goal. But they are more likely to be sensible if it is clear what they are for.

June 1997

Part 3
Inflation

Raising Interest Rates Causes Inflation

OVER THE PAST YEAR the Government has raised interest rates several times, with the aim of reducing inflation. This policy has come under attack by some who claim that far from reducing inflation, raising interest rates will increase it. This claim is a fallacy; and it is this claim we shall deal with here. It must be emphasised that it is only that aspects of criticism of the policy that is addressed – the present article is not concerned with whether the policy reduces inflation, whether it is the best way to reduce inflation, or whether rates have been raised too much or too little.

It is true as a matter of arithmetic that because the interest rate charged on mortgages is in the consumer price index, a rise in the mortgage rate raises inflation, and a fall lowers it. That does mean that if the mortgage rate were dropped from the index, and no other measure of housing costs put in its place, the index would undoubtedly be lower than it is now. But a measure of the cost of living which did not include housing costs would be a pretty poor measure. Some other figure to represent the cost of housing would have to be entered. That would be unlikely to move in steps as the mortgage rate does – so the time path of the consumer price index would be different – probably smoother. But there is nothing to say the index would be any lower; it could well be higher. So that argument for higher interest rates causing inflation is wrong.

There is also another argument. Higher interest rates, it is said, add to firms' costs, and also add to pressure for higher wages. That, it is claimed, is the route by which they cause inflation. The trouble with that argument is that it can be applied to any price. A rise in the price of bananas leaves people with less to spend on other things, just as a rise in interest rates does to those who are net borrowers. Hence one would say that a rise in the price of bananas leads to demand for higher wages, and leads to inflationary pressures. One could go through that argument about the price of every good in the economy. The conclusion would be that a rise in the price of any and every good is a cause of inflation, and thus conclude, not very helpfully, that the cause of inflation is rising prices!

The policy recommendation which follows from this conclusion is that it would be sufficient to prevent inflation that all price increases be forbidden. Notice *sufficient*: on the above argument, nothing else would be necessary! Conversely, cutting prices would reduce inflation! The folly is now at its most transparent. For that policy was tried in the UK; nationalised industries received increased subsidies to hold down prices under the last Labour government and under the Heath administration. Inflation got worse, not better, as these subsidies were financed.

The claim that higher interest rates cause inflation is fallacious; and leads to conclusions and advice even more absurd than the claim itself.

February 1990

Credit Controls Are Better than Interest Rates for Controlling Inflation

AS INTEREST RATES HAVE BEEN RAISED to reduce inflation, it has become increasingly asserted that credit controls would be better, in some way less painful, perhaps also better 'targeted'. These claims are confused. Indeed, they exemplify a failure to understand supply and demand analysis.

Interest rates are raised at times when demand exceeds supply. People are trying to borrow and spend more than others are saving, so the banks expand credit, thus adding to inflationary pressures. There can also be borrowing from overseas, which in these conditions puts downward pressure on the exchange rate and can thus add a once-for-all boost to prices. It seems appealingly simple to say, apply credit controls. Even if these work (very doubtful nowadays) they are not painless or even less painful than interest rates. They are just different.

Existing borrowers do not face higher charges. The burden falls entirely on new borrowers – who cannot get funds at all. They face, in effect, an infinitely high price! It is as if instead of raising rates all round, rates were raised to new borrowers until none wanted to borrow. The idea that credit controls are painless is plainly absurd.

It is sometimes said that it is 'unfair' that existing borrowers have to face higher interest rates than at the start of their loans. This is of course a peculiar idea of fairness – that the burden should fall *entirely* on people who want to borrow after a certain date. And not only does the proposal embody a peculiar idea of fairness – it is also inefficient. It is inefficient in several ways.

First, the scheme is targeted purely according to when the loan is proposed. *Second*, and more important, it works only on borrowers – it does not work on savers. For the purpose of raising rates is to bring borrowing in line with desired savings. Raising saving can help achieve this end. Giving people an incentive to save more works on everyone – people who have not borrowed, existing borrowers and people who are planning to borrow. Credit controls work only on the last of the groups.

In summary, credit controls are not 'fairer' in how they allocate burdens than are higher interest rates. They are just different. With

[43]

regard to efficiency, they are inferior. And all this is based on the assumption, to be discussed in a future 'Fallacy' (pp. 45-6 below), that they can work in a modern open economy.

April 1990

Credit Controls – Do They Work?

IN A PREVIOUS 'ECONOMIC FALLACY EXPOSED' it was shown that contrary to popular claims, credit controls are not a painless way of restricting bank lending. Rather, they just impose pain on different groups from those which would suffer if bank lending was restricted by use of interest rates. That argument was conducted on the basis of assuming that credit controls are actually effective. This column shows that they (credit controls) are, in fact, totally ineffective except in circumstances which we certainly do not welcome.

It should first of all be observed that the evidence that they worked in the past is far from clear-cut. They were usually imposed at times when the economy was booming, and when demands for consumer goods had been growing rapidly. People do not keep adding to their stocks of those goods without limit. What they do is build up a stock of them, and, having done so, use that stock until it is time to replace it. In other words, the demand for consumer goods inevitably has a strong fluctuation to it.

Credit controls were imposed when the demand had been strong for some time, and thus approaching its peak. It was likely that these demands would turn down in any event. That is why it is far from clear that the controls actually worked. But that is not the argument here. This column argues that simply on the grounds of logic such controls can no longer have any significant effect. Suppose that credit controls are imposed. The consequence is initially that some people are denied access to credit and interest rates are lower than they would otherwise be. What happens next? People, including the suppliers of credit, attempt to evade these controls. What means can be used to do so?

An obvious method is to go outside the jurisdiction of those who have imposed the controls – in the present case to go to a foreign country, for example France. Business will be conducted by bankers in France, either British or any other nationality depending simply on who found this area of activity most attractive. This could not be prevented. Banks would, of course, need reserves before they could take deposits and make loans, but these reserves would have to be supplied. If they were not, interest rates would rise in the UK and the purpose of the credit control – restricting credit without raising interest rates – would be entirely frustrated. Accordingly, then, the controls could be evaded very simply by banks and their customers conducting their sterling business outside the UK.

This was not possible in the past, when exchange controls were around Britain. These controls meant that British residents could not conduct their business outside the UK.

It is, of course, the case that some people will be quicker to find the way around controls than others. Controls would impinge most severely on the unsophisticated. This device, to the extent that it works at all, penalises the poor and the uninformed. That is surely not a desirable outcome.

In conclusion, then, exchange controls, if they work, are not painless. But they will not work. They could be evaded simply by going outside the UK. The only kinds of economies which could use exchange controls nowadays, even in principle, are economies such as that which Eastern Europe is moving away from – an economy where private citizens cannot conduct business whenever they deem it in their own interests, with people outside that country. Moving to such an economy would surely be an extremely high price to pay for being able to use a device, credit controls, which is in any event not a painless way of rationing credit but simply a different way from interest rates.

August 1990

An Oil Price Increase Will Cause Inflation

WITH, FIRST, THE OPEC MEETING which agreed to cut oil production so as to raise the oil price, and then the price rise which resulted from the takeover of Kuwait by Iraq, there has been a large number of claims that the rise in the price of oil will raise the inflation rate. There has also been an almost equally large number of calculations of just how much the inflation rate will go up by.

This is a theory of inflation which tells us that the cause of inflation is rising prices. It is a very old theory. All that is new about it is the supposedly precise calculation of just how much a particular price rise will increase inflation. But venerable ancestry does not prevent folly. The theory is ridiculous. If rising prices do cause inflation, why do we not hear accounts of the inflationary consequences of a rise in the price of ice-cream? Or of *Economic Affairs*?

The price of goods has gone up in the past, but this has not imparted a trend to the price level. The price level in Britain was in 1914 *exactly* where it was in 1870. This is only consistent with the theory that inflation is caused by rising prices if no price at all went up in that almost half a century! The theory is plainly incompatible with the facts, despite its current popularity. What is wrong with it? Inflation is a sustained rise in the general level of prices. For a rise in the price of one good to cause that, not only must the price of a good going up raise the general price level, it must keep it going up year after year after year. In fact, it does neither. A rise in the price of a good is a rise in the price relative to the prices of other goods; if the price of one goes up, others can go down – or go up more slowly. Even more important, a *jump* in the price of one good does not produce a continual rise in the prices of all goods.

To believe that a price rise for one good causes all prices to go up, you have to believe that the price of one good relative to another cannot change. And that takes us to the essence of the fallacy. It confuses a relative price, the price of one good relative to another, with the general price level, the price of money in terms of goods in general. A change in the relative price of one good can result only from a change in either demand or supply in the market for that good. The recent oil price rise, a topical example, resulted

[47]

from a restriction in supply, and from fears over future supply affecting demand.

Similarly, a rise in the price level – a fall in the price of money relative to goods – can result only from an increase in the supply of money relative to the demand for it. And an inflation, a sustained fall in the value of money, can result only from an excess supply of money. Believing that a rise in the price of oil will cause inflation involves double confusion.

It confuses a relative price with the general price level. And it confuses a once-for-all change with a continuous change. A rise in the price of any one good does not cause inflation. The only connection it has with inflation is that it gives those in charge of monetary policy a cover for their mistakes.

October 1990

[48]

Devaluation Causes Inflation

IT HAS BECOME INCREASINGLY COMMON in recent months to hear the claim that inflation will rise in this country or that as a result of a currency devaluation. There was concern about that in Britain after Sterling fell out of the ERM. Indeed, various forecasters are still disputing over how much Britain's inflation will be made worse as a result of that event last September; similar discussion has now started in Spain and in Portugal, following the devaluation of the Peseta and the Escudo. And very generally, the claim that devaluation will cause inflation is used as a major argument against devaluation.

Despite that, the claim is wrong. Devaluation may *lead* to inflation; but it can never *cause* inflation.

This is a simple but important distinction that is almost a matter of definition. But although simple and readily understood it is very important in guiding economic policy and in informing discussion of policy.

Inflation is a sustained rise in the general level of prices. A devaluation produces a once-and-for-all reduction in the foreign currency value of a domestic currency. That in turn raises the price of foreign goods relative to domestically produced goods. But just as devaluation produces a one-off decline in the currency's value, so it produces a one-off rise in the price of foreign goods relative to domestic. That need not increase the general level of prices. For it is possible that domestic prices might fall, so that on average prices do not rise. Even if that does not happen, the most that the devaluation can do to the price level of the devaluing country is to raise it once and for all, when the prices of foreign goods rise. It may thus cause an upward step in the price level. That is not an inflation.

It can of course lead to inflation, but that depends on what monetary authorities do, and how wage-rates behave. If the devaluation raises the price level, it makes people worse off. This can lead to claims for higher money wages, to keep their real value – their purchasing power – unchanged. If this happens, the devaluation does not help unemployment fall, for workers are not priced back into jobs. The monetary authorities may be alarmed by unemployment failing to fall. Or, particularly likely, they may be alarmed by unemployment starting to fall, but then rising again as wages go up. They then respond by easing money, and inflation starts to rise.

In other words, a one-off shock to prices can lead to inflation. But it need not. Accordingly, it cannot be said to cause inflation.

Why does such an elementary confusion persist? There are two reasons. One is the perfectly understandable tendency to assume that if one event follows another it is caused by it. The other is that devaluations are quite often the consequence of governments having too expansionary a monetary policy. The consequences of this are concealed until the currency is devalued. And then they appear. Blaming the devaluation – or, quite frequently, the 'speculators' who are asserted to be responsible for it – is then a convenient way for the Government to cover up its own mistakes.

But, whatever the reason for its persistence, the idea that devaluation causes inflation is a fallacy. It causes, at most, a once-and-for-all rise in the price level.

June 1993

Price Rises Above Inflation Are Bad

THERE IS NOW AN ANNUAL RITUAL in London, when fare increases greater than the previous year's inflation are announced for London Transport and British Rail. These increases are denounced for various reasons, *including their being greater than inflation*. The other reasons for objecting to them may be right or wrong; they are not discussed here. The focus of this column is the claim that price increases are bad *because* they are above the rate of inflation.

In one obvious way the objection is just silly. The rate of inflation is an average of price changes. It is almost inevitable that some of these price changes will be above average and some below. (Not quite completely inevitable, because it is possible, though highly unlikely, that every price changes by the same amount; in that case that amount would also be the average price change.) Simply as a matter of arithmetic, then, there is little sense in denouncing price increases because they are above the inflation rate. It is like complaining that some people are above (or below) average height.

There is also another problem, less obvious though at least as important, with objecting to above-inflation – that is, above-average – price rises. Although inflation is measured as an average of price changes, it is fundamentally different from any individual price change. Inflation is a fall in the purchasing power of money, or a rise in the level of prices *in general*. An individual price change is a change in what is called a *relative price* – the price of one good compared to other goods. We measure relative prices in money, but the information they actually convey is how much of one good you have to give up to buy another good (or other goods).

Changes in these relative prices affect both production and consumption. They affect the allocation of resources, by changing incentives to supply goods, and incentives to buy them. Price changes of this sort are useful. In contrast, inflation brings no benefits (although it does help the government to raise revenue).

Hence a price rise above the inflation rate – that is to say, above average – signals that there is a shortage of that good relative to others. The price rise reduces incentives to consume the good and increases incentives to supply it. Price rises below the rate of inflation would send the opposite signals.

Seeing relative prices moving around is in general the symptom of a healthy economy, with innovation going on in production techniques and people's tastes changing in response to increasing prosperity. These price changes can also be bad news, of course, for consumers – an example was the increase in oil prices of some years ago. But even such changes, although unwelcome for some, serve a purpose: they induce consumers to reduce consumption of the good, and to look for substitutes.

It is now possible to draw the above points together. By the nature of the definition of inflation, some price rises must be above inflation and some below. More important, the price changes of individual goods are relative price changes; in contrast, inflation is a fall in the value of money. The former serves a useful purpose, while the latter does not. Indeed, inflation actually impedes the resource-allocating task of relative price changes. For if the average price level is steady – zero inflation – then it is clear that all price changes are relative price changes, to be responded to accordingly. If there is inflation, then it becomes necessary to sort out the extent to which the price change of a good is a price change relative to other goods, and how much is a change in the value of the good relative to money. Only the first part of the price change is a signal to reallocate production and consumption.

If there were no inflation at all, any price rise would be above the rate of inflation. There might well be reasons for complaining about such a price rise, but that it was above the inflation rate would not be one. Complaining on these grounds entails two errors. It shows that there is neither understanding of the definition of inflation, nor understanding of the vital role of relative prices in an economy.

February 1994

Relative Price Changes Can Be Ignored

RECENTLY A CHARITY DREW ATTENTION to the plight of poor children by arguing that children whose parents were supported by the state were actually worse off than in Victorian times. The claim was that it would cost more than the allowance given for children now to buy the diet which was supplied in Dr. Barnardo's homes in the 19th century.

This betrays a misunderstanding of the nature of price indices; these indices are used for two purposes. *First*, they provide a measure of price changes of goods in general over time – or of the change over time in the value of money. *Second*, they are used to calculate how 'real' variables – physical quantities – have changed over time. For example, if national income in money terms has doubled, we do not know whether people are better off until we have corrected for any change in prices (that is, 'deflated' it by the price index).

That price index represents the cost of buying a bundle of goods. But it is not a constant bundle of goods. Its physical composition changes over time, for two reasons. Some goods simply disappear from production, or at any rate from widespread use – horse-drawn carriages and candles are examples. They are replaced by other things – in these cases by motor transport and electric light. Others disappear, or have their importance in the index reduced, because of changes in price relative to other goods. If a good becomes more expensive relative to some substitute, consumption of it falls while consumption of the substitute rises.

Not allowing for this by changing the composition of the index would be misleading because the index would no longer reflect what people actually spend their money on, but what they *used* to spend their money on.

When a good disappears from use because it is obsolete (a horse-drawn carriage) we do not, when calculating a price index, pretend it has not disappeared. Similarly, if a good that had disappeared from consumption because of a price change were kept in the index, we would be measuring the price of a bundle of goods no longer consumed.

Reduced use may appear different – it may seem 'unfair' that people can no longer afford to buy something. But that view

[53]

neglects the importance of changing relative prices in our economy. They reflect changing relative scarcities. As a good becomes scarce, its price rises, and people are thus induced to look for a substitute. The price system encourages us to economise on scarce resources, and to seek more abundant substitutes, thus maintaining economic efficiency by reducing wastefulness.

Of course, it can seem unfair that the poor may have to pay more heed to those changes than the rich. And it can seem foolish, infuriatingly so on occasions, if a price rise is the result of a misconceived government policy. But to object to the price index on these grounds is to complain about the messenger, not the message.

The price of food is an interesting case. There have been major changes in relative prices not just over the past century, but over much shorter time-periods. Within living memory, chicken has moved from a delicacy to a readily available fairly cheap dish. And over a longer period, oysters have moved from abundance to being a delicacy.

Relative prices change the set of goods which people consume, and this change in turn changes the price index. Compilers of indices thus have a choice. They can either track the price of an underlying bundle of goods, or of a bundle of goods which a 'representative person' buys. The latter has to be interpreted carefully, but it is nevertheless more generally useful than the former. For the former would be substantially influenced by goods consumed in small quantities, or even not consumed at all, because their prices had gone up so much. The information would be accurate but not very interesting. The charity which calculated the price of a particular bundle of goods over a century thus fell into a trap which is often laid by economic data. You can get a precise measure, or a rough-and-ready one. The precise one, however, may give very little information, while the approximation can be very informative when used carefully.

A price index that does not incorporate the effect on behaviour of relative price changes ignores people's response to price signals and thus gives one very precisely a piece of almost useless information. Ignoring the effects of relative price changes is always a mistake in economics. The construction of price indices is no exception to that rule. The information that the food consumed by children in Barnardo's in the 19th century would now cost more to buy than an allowance given for the support of children today tells us nothing about children's well-being – because the calculation on which it is based ignores relative price changes.

April 1994

Part 4

Fiscal Policy, Investment and Taxes

Governments Can Precisely Manage the Economy by Fiscal Policy

WITH THE LATEST BUDGET we again heard cries that the Chancellor should 'take some more out of the economy', that taxes should go higher, usually to raise some precisely specified amount of revenue, and so have a precisely specified effect on aggregate demand. Had the economy been in recession, we would no doubt have heard exactly the opposite recommendations, couched in exactly the same language.

The idea is nonsense. The Government's tax and spending policies do affect the economy. But their effect on demand is primarily in its *composition*. To the extent that they affect the *level* of demand, the effect is uncertain both in size and duration.

To see this, consider the current situation. The Government was running a surplus, its revenue exceeded its expenditure. This meant it was repaying debt. The instruction to 'take more out of the economy' meant repay more debt. In other words, someone would pay more taxes to the Government so that the Government would redeem debt held by someone else. Person A's disposable income would have been reduced so that person B's capital could be converted from bonds to a bank deposit.

Now, how is that supposed to affect demand? The effect on A's spending is not precisely known. If he expects taxes to be lower in the future – as a result of lower debt service costs – he will not cut back his spending by the full amount of his tax increase.

And what of person B? What happens to his savings? They will be spent. Or they will be lent to somebody else, who assuredly does not borrow them with the intention of not spending them. If they are left in a bank deposit, they will be lent to a spender – by the bank.

There will of course be delays. Person B may take some time to think what to do. His borrower may take some time to spend. During such delays, spending will dip. But only during the adjustment period. And how long this will be, no one can say.

In summary, fiscal policy relies on lags in adjustment. These are lags whose length we can neither explain nor predict. Fine tuning by fiscal policy is impossible.

Recommending it presumes more knowledge about the economy than we have now and are ever likely to have.

June 1990

Government Can Decide Who Pays a Tax

'Labor Leaders Demanded Changes in the Senate Health-Care Bill'

'Of particular concern is a provision…that would require employers to pay only 50% of their workers' insurance costs – rather than the 80% share first proposed by the administration.'

THE ABOVE QUOTATION, from the *Wall Street Journal* of 5 August 1994, exemplifies a very common fallacy which is also found in Britain. But while governments can impose taxes, and can insist they be paid, they have no power whatsoever to determine who will pay the tax, or any particular share of it.

The division of the burden depends on conditions in the market for the good or service that is being taxed, and not on the government.

Imagine a world (Oh happy world!) with no taxes. In such a setting, the price consumers paid for a good would be received *in its entirety* by the suppliers of the good. There is no gap between the 'demand price' (what the consumer pays) and the 'supply price' (what the producer receives).

Now the government decides to put a tax on that good. This introduces a third party into the transaction. That third party wants a share of what is being paid over by the consumer. Who (seller or buyer) pays that share?

Suppose first that the supplier simply adds the tax to his selling price. Consumers will usually react to this by buying a smaller amount than before of the good. This in turn affects the price the supplier requires per unit of the good (the supply price). The more of a good that is supplied beyond a certain amount, the more the producers require per unit to supply it. And, of course, conversely, when output falls, supply price per unit falls. Hence when the tax is imposed, consumers buy less of the good as the price to them rises, and as producers are now producing less of it, the supply price falls.

So in general, when a tax is imposed on a good (or a service) four things happen. The price paid by consumers rises; the price received by producers falls; the government takes the difference between what the consumer pays and what the producer receives; and the quantity sold falls.

Sometimes the price received by the producer does not fall; this is so if costs of production do not vary with output. But quantity sold still falls, so the producer still suffers as a result of the imposition of the tax.

There is one case, and one case only, where neither the price the producer receives, nor the quantity he sells, changes as a result of the tax. This is when consumers' demand is totally insensitive to price – a rare (possibly non-existent) case.

So far, then, we can see that once the government legislates for the tax, the usual case is that both consumers and producers contribute to paying it. This contribution is not affected by a statute which says who is legally responsible for handing over the money. The respective contributions of consumers and producers to the tax are determined by how sensitive consumers' demand is to changes in price, and by the extent to which the price at which producers sell varies with their production rate.

So far the discussion has been of a market for goods. The same conclusion holds in the market for labour. As the costs of workers rise, employers will employ fewer. Meanwhile, looking at the supply side, more will have to be paid to tempt more workers into an industry. Accordingly, when the government imposes a tax which creates a gap between what employers pay and what employees receive, part of the tax is paid by employers and part by employees, regardless of what the legislation says. Further, the part each pays is entirely unaffected by any legislation over the share each pays. The wage the employer pays rises; the wage the employee receives falls; and the gap goes to the government.

How does this accord with the fact that when a worker looks at his pay slip, he sees a total from which certain deductions, including what the government has legislated he will pay, have been made? The answer is that, at any rate after a period of adjustment to a tax, bargaining really takes place over *after-tax* wages. Employers know they have to add something to, and employees know they have to subtract something from, the *before-tax* figure. It is that bargaining, not legislation, which brings the responsiveness of demand and supply to price into play, and in turn

[62]

that determines how much costs rise to the employer and how much earnings by workers fall.

Legislating for who bears what share of a tax is as pointless as legislating how many hours per day the sun will shine.

November 1994

The Chancellor Cannot Afford to Cut Taxes
Since the PSBR Is Overshooting its Target

THE ABOVE QUOTATION paraphrases a conclusion reached by an increasing number of commentators recently. It embodies in fact a good number of fallacies. But before dealing with them, a definition will be useful.

The PSBR is the Public Sector Borrowing Requirement. That is, broadly speaking, the difference between what the government spends and what it takes from the private sector by taxation. It is, in other words, what the government has to borrow to pay for all its spending. The Government is spending about 42 per cent of national income this year and is aiming at a PSBR equal to about 3-4 per cent of GNP. Hence the PSBR is the difference between two large numbers, both of which, tax revenue and government spending, are hard to forecast.

Errors in forecasts are therefore easy. When one adds to that the fact that neither tax revenues nor tax receipts flow smoothly through the year, but rather fluctuate very substantially indeed from month to month, we can see the folly of making strong claims as to the precise size of the PSBR only a little way beyond the mid-point of the financial year. There we see the first fallacy – believing forecasts whose claims to accuracy are without any foundation. (That is a fallacy which affects more forecasts than just those for the PSBR, but that is another matter.)

Moving on, why is the PSBR going to exceed the Chancellor's objective? (Accepting for the sake of discussion that it probably is, although by an unpredictable amount.) It is doing so primarily because the economy is growing more slowly than expected. This reduces tax revenues, because incomes and expenditure, and hence receipts from taxes on them, are growing more slowly than expected. It also tends to increase some categories of spending, such as social security. (Note that this slow growth cannot excuse the failure of some ministers to control budgets essentially unaffected by the state of the economy.) We know that unexpectedly slow growth of the economy is contributing to the PSBR overshoot because the Chancellor published growth forecasts both in his November 1994 Budget and again earlier this year.

[64]

Now we come to another peculiarity in the above quotation. Many of the commentators now saying that taxes cannot be cut because the PSBR is overshooting would only a few years ago have been panicking that the economy was slowing, and clamouring for tax cuts to 'get it going again'. How fickle are unthinking followers of fashion, and not just when buying clothes.

Finally we come to the most basic fallacy in the quotation. To see it, consider first why the Chancellor is concerned with the size of the PSBR. Government borrowing adds to the stock of government debt outstanding. If the stock of debt is rising faster than national income, then the cost of debt service will rise as a share of national income. This will push up taxes, and has in the past also led governments to inflate. Hence too fast growth of debt is to be shunned. There is also the possibility of a 'virtuous circle'. If the stock of debt is falling relative to national income, then so is the cost of debt service, and so in turn can there be cuts in taxes.

The Chancellor's concern, then, is, quite properly, with the *long-run* behaviour of the PSBR – with how it will behave on average over a period of years. He is not alarmed by increases in the PSBR produced by a slowing economy, nor should he be elated by falls in the PSBR produced by an accelerating economy. The objective of policy, properly understood, is what is sometimes called the 'cyclically adjusted PSBR'. That is what the PSBR would be, given tax rates and spending plans, if the economy were growing at its trend rate.

To summarise so far, then, the Chancellor is concerned with the long-run behaviour of the PSBR. Fluctuations around that long run produced by fluctuations in the economy are of no concern at all, at least in principle.

Now, that last phrase does conceal considerable problems. These arise because of the difficulty of judging where the economy's trend actually is, and of trying to work out what tax revenue and spending would be when at the trend. Doing that is not easy. We can look back and estimate what the trend has been. But when we do so, it appears that the trend has changed from time to time, and usually for no obvious reason. Further, the problem is increased just at the moment by the period of turbulence which resulted first from the Lawson boom, and then from the recession produced to squeeze the inflation that boom produced; so although

[65]

the Chancellor has quite correctly got a long-run PSBR target, it is not easy for him to work out how far away he is from it.

But despite these practical difficulties, the principle is clear. The current behaviour of the PSBR, its deviation from its planned path, is due in part to the economy not behaving as was expected. That deviation should not affect in any way the Chancellor's long-run tax and spending plans. Claims that it should reveal a profound misunderstanding of why the Chancellor has a PSBR target.

There are all sorts of other questions – for example, is his long-run PSBR target the correct one? But, to summarise the main issues, the Chancellor has chosen a long-run PSBR target. He was correct to do so. He should not change his plans for achieving it because of a temporary fluctuation in the economy away from its trend. The advice that he should do so is fallacious, just as was the advice often given in the past (by the same people to a considerable extent) that if the economy is slowing taxes should be cut or spending increased without regard to the long-run consequences for the PSBR. Those who tender such advice have leapt from one fallacy to another without pausing even for a moment on a sensible conclusion.

December 1995

Employers Contribute Towards Workers' Benefits

A LABOUR PARTY SPOKESMAN recently declared that, whatever changes the Labour Party was considering in the scope or rates of National Insurance Contributions, an employer's contribution would be retained. The reason given for this was that by levying that contribution, it was ensured that employers contributed towards health and retirement benefits for those they employed.

This is an example of a very old and very common economic fallacy. Believing it is certainly not confined to Labour Party spokesmen. Examples could be found in any country, and from every political party. The example noted above is simply a recent one.

The fallacy is to believe that the government has any ability whatsoever to control who bears the burden of a tax.

To avoid confusion it should be said explicitly that for the purposes of this analysis National Insurance is like a tax, in that it is a compulsory levy charged by government – on income in this case. It differs from other taxes in that it is purportedly allocated to the provision of certain specified benefits, but that distinction is not relevant for this present purpose. What matters here is that it is, like income tax, a compulsory charge on income. It does, however, differ from income tax in that part of it is 'paid' by the employer. That might seem to settle the question. The employer is obliged to pay it by law; so that is their contribution. But that is not the case.

National insurance contributions, be they 'employers" or 'employees", like income tax, create a gap between what the employer pays and what the employee receives. In the absence of all taxes and other compulsory charges on income, the employer's average costs per worker and a worker's earnings would be the same. But compulsory payments change that situation. Suppose the law is that of every £100 the worker earns, he can keep £90, and £10 goes to the government. The law could say that he first gets his £100 and has to hand over £10 – the employee has the legal liability to pay; or it could say that the £10 is deducted by the employer before each £100 is handed over – the employer has the legal liability to pay. Now, what does the assignment of legal liability affect? It affects neither the fact that if the employee wants to keep £100, he has to earn more than that; nor the fact that if the employer wants £100 worth of work supplied, he has to pay more than £100.

So the first, and fundamental, point is that the charge increases the cost of obtaining labour; and also means that to earn £100, more than £100 worth of labour has to be supplied. Seeing that leads on to discuss who bears the cost, and why.

Think for simplicity of a situation with one worker and one employer. The worker can vary the hours he works, and the employer can choose to buy a variable amount of hours. Other things equal, we would expect the worker to be willing to work more hours the more he was paid per hour. Similarly, the less each hour of work cost, the more of them would the employer buy.

The worker and his employer would negotiate, and discover that at some wage rate the amount of hours the worker was willing to work equalled the amount the employer wanted to buy at that wage rate. That would be the wage rate agreed, and the hours worked would be what the employer and employee both wanted at that rate of pay per hour. That can be called the 'pre-tax equilibrium' situation. Now suppose a tax is imposed. Continuing with the above numbers, suppose the tax is at a 10 per cent flat rate; for any £100 earned, £10 tax is paid. Initially (if a contract of any reasonable duration exists between employer and employee) nothing changes. The employee works the same number of hours as before, receives the same payment as before, and 10 per cent of that payment is handed over.

Notice that even at this stage, before renegotiation, where the legal burden to pay the tax over lies is immaterial. The employer pays a certain amount, and the employee keeps 90 per cent of that amount. This is true whether the wage is paid over before or after the tax is deducted. But that situation is not an equilibrium. Nothing has changed for the employer; but the employee is getting less pay per hour than before. If content before, he certainly is not content now. As soon as allowed under the contract, renegotiation will take place. The employee will wish to work somewhat fewer hours, at a higher rate per hour (since he keeps less of what he earns); and since more is being demanded per hour, the employer will wish to buy fewer hours. Eventually, a new situation, the 'post-tax equilibrium', will be reached. Fewer hours of work will be supplied, and a higher wage rate per hour will be paid.

There will be a change in the amount earned before tax, and 10 per cent of this changed amount will be handed over as tax. None of this is affected by where the legal burden to pay the tax is placed. What has happened is that a gap has been created between what the employer pays and what the employee receives; wage costs now exceed earnings. This leads the employer to cut back demand, and the employee to cut back supply. By how much is each cut back? This depends on how sensitive each is to changes in price. The more sensitive, the greater will be the change in supply or in demand.

The 'cost' of the tax is thus shared between employer and employee. The employee earns less per hour and works fewer hours; the employer pays more per hour, but employs the worker for fewer hours. The distribution of these changes depends solely on respective sensitivity to wage changes of employer's demand and employee's supply, and on nothing else. Where the legal obligation lies is immaterial.

The above description can of course be extended to a situation with many employers and many employees. Here hours worked might vary; and numbers employed would almost certainly also change. But the crucial characteristics of the post-tax equilibrium would be unchanged. Every hour of work would cost employers more than workers received for it. The gap would be tax.

The introduction of the tax would reduce demand for workers, and reduce willingness to work. How the burden was shared would depend on no legal obligation; but on sensitivity of demand and supply to changes in wage rates.

Claiming the fact that the law says a particular person or group pays a tax determines who pays it, is a fallacy. The location of the legal obligation to hand over the money to the government is immaterial in determining who bears the tax. Government can no more legislate for that than it can legislate for the sun always to shine at Wimbledon.

September 1996

[69]

Investment Is a Good Thing, and Should Be Encouraged by Every Means in the Government's Power

EXHORTATIONS TO INVEST more are common. Opposition parties (in every country) are habitually accusing governments of 'underinvesting' in this or that. Sometimes the criticism is truly fatuous, and governments are urged to 'invest more in our future' – as if we could invest in the past, perhaps in last year or last century. But even when that particular stupidity is not perpetrated, the advice to invest more is not necessarily sound.

People can spend their incomes on the consumption of goods and services, or they can save. Before there can be investment there has to be saving. Investment, in other words, is *deferred consumption*.

It may have been deferred so that more can be consumed later. It may have been deferred simply to enable there to *be* consumption later – an important reason for saving by individuals with volatile incomes. Or it may have been deferred so that it can augment the consumption of future generations by being bequeathed to descendants.

But whatever the motive (except in the rare case of the individual who accumulates savings simply for the pleasure of accumulation and with no other end in view) saving, and hence investment, is not an end in itself. It is a means of achieving an end. Therefore in turn it is only desirable to increase investment if doing so furthers the achievement of that end, and does so at a price worth paying.

In other words, the return on the investment is of great importance. When politicians urge more investment, they should think both about what the return on it will be, and what is being given up by that investment. Does the benefit of the return exceed the benefit that would have come from what has to be given up? That is the crucial question, and despite being crucial it is often ignored.

We frequently hear it claimed that Britain is investing too little in this or that compared to 'overseas competition'. (The notion that countries rather than firms compete with one another is also a fallacy, and has been dealt with on pages 36-38.) But looking at the amount invested in different countries, and saying we should increase ours to that of the highest, is simply wrong. For the costs of investing elsewhere may be lower, or the returns higher, or both. It can be worth investigating, and is always worth thinking about, why investment (relative to, say, income) differs in different countries. But the simple fact of difference in itself can justify only that investigation. It cannot justify trying to increase investment forthwith.

This is the more so because, starting from the notion that investment is a desirable end in itself, calling something investment is then thought to justify expenditure on it with no more ado. The concept of investment in education is an interesting example. We are told to 'invest more in education'. What does this mean? It has been applied, for example, to increasing the salaries of school teachers. Now, there may or may not be a case for that. But increasing the wages of providers of services is about as far away from investment – that is to say, the purchase of a durable asset which provides a stream of service in the future – as we can get!

There are also claims, derived from some modern theories of the causes of economic growth, that investment will raise an economy's growth rate. By this is meant not just that it can temporarily boost demand, but that it can produce a sustainable rise in the rate of increase per head. If achievable, that is certainly desirable. This modern growth theory can support such claims; but in a very precise way, not the broad-brush way in which it has been seized on by advocates of increased state intervention in the economy. The theory essentially says that certain types of investment may need to be encouraged to raise an economy's growth rate because they provide generalised benefits – benefits which do not accrue only to the investor. The theory does not say that raising any type of investment by subsidy from the general body of taxpayers will raise the growth rate.

To conclude, the basic fallacy behind the claim that we should invest more is to confuse outputs and inputs, ends and means. Investment is the deferral of the ultimate aim of economic activity, consumption. It is therefore a cost.

No-one has yet claimed – to my knowledge anyway – that if one uses lots of labour as compared with another firm or country to produce some good then that is desirable. Exactly the same applies to investment. Investment is a cost of production. We should invest as efficiently as possible, not as much as possible.

December 1996

Taxes Should Go Up to Slow Inflation

IN THE SPRING AND EARLY SUMMER of 1997, almost every commentator on the British economy (with the notable exception of Samuel Brittan) argued that inflation in Britain was starting to accelerate, and that taxes should be raised (or public spending cut) to stop it. Now, it may or may not be case that inflation was accelerating; and there may or may not have been a case for raising taxes or cutting spending so as to reduce government borrowing. Neither of these points is considered here. The focus is on the claim that a rise in taxes will slow inflation. That claim is a fallacy, but a somewhat complex one, in that there is one set of extraordinary circumstances where it is justified. Those circumstances are discussed briefly below. But in general, and certainly in Britain today, a rise in taxes does not stop inflation. That point can be made first by analysis and then reinforced by evidence.

A useful starting point is a definition of inflation. Inflation is a long-lasting rise in the general level of prices. It is a rise which goes on until something changes to stop it. This is in contrast to a change in the price level, which is a move from one price level to another, at which the price level then stays.

The fact that inflation is a continuous process should immediately make one pause before claiming that a rise in taxes will stop it. Unless the price level is like an imaginary frictionless ball on an imaginary frictionless (and infinitely large) billiard table – in which case one tap would sent it moving forever – for inflation one should look for a cause that is present so long as the inflation is present. One should look for a *continuous cause for a continuous process*.

It might be claimed that a tax increase *would* remove a continuous cause, for the cause is 'excess demand' – demand greater than can be supplied without upward price pressure. Can a tax increase do that? What is to be done with the tax revenue? If it is not to be spent by its recipient, the government, then it will reduce government borrowing, lead to debt repayment, or, in the extraordinary case where a government not only is not borrowing but has no debts to repay, to the government acquiring assets.

[73]

Consider the expenditure consequences of each of these in turn. If less is borrowed, then the money which was to be lent will be lent or spent elsewhere. It will not just vanish. If the taxes are used to repay existing debts, then the recipient of the repayment will in turn do something with it – lend (to someone who will spend) – or spend directly. (Of course no-one would claim that the pattern of spending will not be affected, but that is a different matter.) And exactly the same applies to the acquisition of assets. If these are acquired from the domestic private sector, the recipients have money to spend.

It might be objected at this point that the above arguments seem to deny the existence, even in principle, of the Keynesian 'multiplier'. That, it may be recollected, claimed to show that (for example) a rise in government spending financed by a rise in taxes would lead to an increase in total spending, as private expenditure would fall by less than the rise in taxes. How can that be?

People must somehow cut their expenditure by less than the rise in taxes – which they can only do by saving less. What happens to the people who were borrowing those savings? They will be unable to spend. This does not end up reducing private spending by as much as the rise in government spending goes up only if that private saving was somehow sitting there unused – a possibility perhaps in a depression, with the price level actually falling so that people defer spending in the expectation that 'prices will be lower tomorrow'. But we are not dealing with that, but with the problem of *inflation*; so that special case need not be considered further.

So far, then, it has been argued that there are two problems with the claim that a rise in taxes will slow inflation. *First*, inflation is a continuous process but a rise in taxes is a one-off cause, so it is hard to argue that the latter will stop the former. *Second*, the effects of a rise in taxes on private sector spending have been considered, and it has been shown that certainly in an environment of strong demand and rising prices, a rise in taxes cannot be expected to reduce total spending, by the government and the private sector combined, in the economy (although it may well change its composition).

So much for analysis. What about evidence? The evidence goes the same way. The effects of tax increases on spending are uncertain – uncertain both in size and in timing. Evidence can be drawn both from the UK and overseas. First, the UK. In 1967 fiscal policy was tightened after a devaluation. There was no balance-of-payments effect. That only came when domestic demand was squeezed by a monetary tightening. Looking further back in history, we find inflation rising and falling with no associated changes in taxes: for example, prices fell on average from 1870 to the early 1890s, and then rose steadily to 1914. But there was no matching change (or even series of changes) in taxes. And in the USA, in the late 1960s, a tax increase was imposed but inflation continued until monetary policy was tightened.

In short, the evidence does not suggest that in general a fiscal tightening is necessary *or* sufficient to slow inflation. What of the special case mentioned earlier? This is when governments are financing their expenditure by money creation rather than by taxing or borrowing. Almost every hyperinflation – an inflation greater than 50 per cent per month – has resulted from such behaviour. Tax increases to stop money creation would then be necessary to stop the hyperinflation. But governments have generally got into that situation because they had lost the political support to let them raise taxes – so the recommendation is desirable but not possible.

In normal times a tax increase (or a spending cut) might, via reducing government borrowing, reduce interest rates, and this might induce people to hold more money, thus reducing the excess of money supply over money demand. But this would be a once only effect on the excess *stock* of money; to slow inflation a fall in the *rate of growth* of excess money is necessary.

To conclude, the claim that a rise in taxes will slow inflation is without analytical foundation (except in the case of hyperinflation) and is inconsistent with the facts. There is therefore absolutely no reason why taxes in Britain should go up to slow inflation.

September 1997

[75]

Part 5

Monetary Policy and Banking

High Interest Rates Are Bad for the Economy, and the Government Should Reduce Them Forthwith

THE INTEREST RATE IS A PRICE. It is the price borrowers pay and the price savers receive. If we are to understand the consequences of a price – any price – being 'high' (which presumably means higher than average), we have to understand why it is high.

An example is useful. There is a rise in the price of bananas relative to other fruit. What will happen to sales of bananas? The answer is that we cannot say until we know why the price has risen.

It may have risen because there has been a cut-back in supply – as a result of a bad harvest. In this case, sales will fall, and the rise in price will have served to cut back the quantity demanded to the temporarily reduced amount available.

But the price could equally well have gone up because there was an increase in demand – because of change in tastes produced, say, by the discovery that bananas were exceptionally good for you. In this case, the increase in price accompanies an increase in sales – and if it persists will encourage increased investment in banana production.

The same argument applies to the interest rate. To understand the consequences of change in that price, just as in the case of the banana price, we have to understand the reason it has gone up. Traditionally, over more than 200 years, high interest rates have coincided with wars. They have been drawn up by demand to use resources in the present, rather than to invest them for future production. Less dramatic, but also clear, is the tendency for interest rates to rise and fall with the level of economic activity. Traditionally, rates have been pulled up by demand for resources. High interest rates are traditionally associated with high investment. They are the result of surges in the demand for funds to invest.

Why, then, the present concern to reduce interest rates to avoid harming investment? Partly, no doubt, they are the result of the quite reasonable desire of manufacturers (and all other borrowers) to see their costs fall. (It is perhaps a little surprising that calls by savers for higher interest rates are not equally common.) But also, and very important, is the reason interest rates are high. They have been pulled up by buoyant demand in the UK. And they have been pushed up by the authorities – the Bank of England acting at the behest of the government – to reduce money growth and thereby slow inflation.

That leads to two fresh questions. Which interest rates have they pulled up, and what was the alternative? The first entails long discussion, and is for another day. The second must be dealt with now.

If the authorities had not pushed up interest rates, what would have happened? Inflation would have accelerated, rising rapidly from the 5-6 per cent range and shooting into the teens. So that was the choice. Higher interest rates for a time, or accelerating inflation.

When that is understood, the fallacy involved in always complaining about high interest rates is clear. *First*, it matters why they are high – sometimes they are a sign of healthy economic growth. *Second*, choices cannot be evaluated one at a time; the available alternative has to be considered. If the authorities pushed down rates now, we would have spiralling inflation.

High interest rates are far from always bad; and at the moment, it would be folly to push rates down.

December 1988

International Capital Mobility Has Increased, So Governments Have Little Control Over Economic Activity

IT IS COMMONLY CLAIMED in broadcasts, in newspaper correspondence columns, sometimes in articles on economics, that as a result of increased capital mobility the scope for a government to affect the course of the national economy is much reduced. Sometimes this is seen as good, sometimes bad; sometimes it is used as part of a case for European monetary union. And sometimes, and most worryingly, it is used as the basis of a case for restrictions on international capital movements.

But regardless of how the assertion is used, the fact is that it is totally wrong. International capital mobility can restrict a government's freedom of action. But it need not. Whether or not capital flows constrain government policy is a matter for the government's own choice. The circumstances under which they do constrain policy, and those in which they do not, are easily set out and contrasted.

Suppose first that a country is in a genuine fixed exchange rate system. The exchange rate of its currency is fixed against some other currency or currencies, and will not change. (A good example of such a situation is the relationship between English and Scottish pounds.) In such a setting, let the monetary authorities in one country try to ease monetary policy. An inevitable consequence of this is that short-term interest rates drop. When that happens, those who have funds in that country will move them to the other. There is, after all, no exchange risk, and a higher interest rate is on offer. Money will flow from one country to the other – tightening policy in the country which has eased, easing it in the country which has not. The overall effect on policy in the two countries cannot be specified in general; it depends on such factors as the relative size of the two countries, and on which is seen as 'the leader' in the conduct of monetary policy. But except in the special case where the country which has eased is the leader, and the other country follows, it is clear that in this set-up capital flows do constrain national monetary policies.

Now we look at the opposite case – of a freely floating exchange rate between the two economies. Once again, one country eases monetary policy and its interest rates fall. People try to move their capital. But this time the exchange rate is depressed by their doing so; indeed, it is highly likely to drop in anticipation. The exchange rate will in principle adjust until the expected return is the same in both currencies, and there will be no flow of money.

So in this second case, the monetary easing is *reinforced* by an exchange rate depreciation. It is not offset by a drain of money overseas.

Now, governments can choose whether to have a fixed exchange rate or a floating one. If they have a floating rate, then monetary policy is not constrained by international capital mobility. If they have a fixed exchange rate, then policy is so constrained. But there should be no complaint about that for it is a well-known consequence of fixed exchange rates.

In summary, capital flows can constrain national economic policies – but only if governments want them to.

September 1992

Rising Bond Yields Will Slow the Economy

IN THE SPRING AND EARLY SUMMER OF 1994, long-term interest rates – yields on government bonds – rose sharply, not just in Britain, but all around the world (although to different extents). Everywhere there was discussion of the consequences. In some countries it was argued that the rise meant the central bank need not tighten monetary policy to slow the economy. In others, there were fears the rise would prolong recessions which previously had appeared to be ending. In any event, there seemed to be a consensus that the rise would affect the economy, so as to slow down or reverse economic growth to at least a modest extent.

There was also some rather limited discussion of why the rise had occurred, but curiously no one linked it with discussion of the consequence of the rise. That is a pity, for if they had they might have reached rather different conclusions.

The return on long-term government bonds has two parts – the real rate of interest and the expected rate of inflation over the life of the bond. The two sum to make the interest rate on the bond. The first component is the return in real terms that lenders receive. It is the payment they get for abstaining from consumption now, the increase in future purchasing power they obtain for lending out their money rather than spending it. This return is unaffected by inflation. It could, indeed, actually be paid in physical units of whatever the money borrowed is used to produce. Usually it is not, but that is only because it is convenient in a money-using economy to be paid in money rather than, say, in bicycles or wine. The return reflects a genuine increase in purchasing power as a result of having saved and lent out the saving. Borrowers are willing to pay that return because they judge that, by borrowing and spending, they get a return which compensates them for the payments they made to the lender. Thus the real rate is determined by the supply of savings and the demand for funds to invest. If people become more willing to save, the real rate will fall; and vice versa. As for borrowers, if they see more or better investment projects, they will bid up the real rate; however, should attractive investment projects become more rare, the real rate will fall.

In other words, the real rate of interest is a price which moves in response to changes in the desire to consume now relative to consuming later, and in response to changes in demand for funds to invest.

What about expected inflation? Lenders will want compensation for any fall in the value of money they think will occur over the period of the loan. Otherwise, the money they get back in the future would not buy what it could when they lent it out – they could end up worse off as a result of saving. Should lenders not demand this compensation, borrowers would enjoy a windfall by borrowing at a negative real interest rate.

Where does this lead for the rise in bond yields? They can have risen for two reasons. Either the real rate or expected inflation has gone up (or a bit of both). What are the consequences for the economy?

If real rates have gone up, there is a change in demand relative to supply for consumption goods or investment goods. There is no reason why this should affect the *total* of economic activity. It would certainly affect the *composition* of output, and there might be a temporary dip in the total while resources moved from one area of activity to another. But there is no reason why such a rise should have more than a very temporary effect on economic activity.

What about expected inflation? If expected inflation increases, people will switch from assets which are vulnerable to inflation into ones which offer some form of protection against it. They will, for example, switch out of currency and bank accounts which do not pay interest. What effect will this have on the economy? To the extent that it is noticeable, it will boost demand, for there will be an increase – perhaps temporary – in the demand for the goods. In summary, there is no reason for an increase in bond yields to slow the economy. The fallacy arises from forgetting that a bond yield is a price. One can never discuss the consequences of a price change without knowing why it has happened. Prices change in response to changes in the economy. Only when it is known what these changes are can the consequences of the resulting price movement sensibly be discussed. Changes in bond yields – or in any other price – have effects on the economy which depend on the cause of the price change. Prices reflect what is happening in the economy. Forgetting that can lead to accepting as true the fallacy that changing bond yields affect economic activity. Treating other

[84]

prices that way can also lead to accepting many other fallacies; but those are for another day.

October 1994

The Bank of England Should Rescue a Failed or Failing Bank

A COMMON FALLACY, given fresh life recently by the failure of Barings, is that a central bank has a duty, in its role as lender of last resort, to rescue a bank which has failed or is just about to fail. In fact, central banks *never* should do that and seldom *could* do so. Claiming that they should misunderstands the central bank's responsibility as 'lender of last resort'.

This task (whose naming, interestingly, is usually credited to Sir Francis Baring in 1797) arises because central banks now have a monopoly over the note issue, and of the supply of deposits at the central bank – two ultimate means of settlement in a monetary system and the medium of exchange in which confidence remains after it has been lost in all others. If confidence is lost in central bank money, the whole monetary system breaks down.

Banks hold only a small portion of reserves against their liabilities. They take deposits, and lend out the majority of them. Only a small fraction is retained as cash or its equivalent, a deposit at the central bank. Thus it is possible – though unlikely – that a bank will run out of cash if withdrawals exceed deposits. A bank's first recourse in such an event is to borrow from other banks. Usually it can do so without difficulty, for one bank's excess of withdrawals over deposits implies an excess of deposits over withdrawals for the rest of the system.

But occasionally this has not been possible. Such episodes usually happened immediately after a bank failed – as a result, say, of incompetence, bad luck or even fraud. Depositors in the bank usually lost some or all of their deposits. Seeing depositors at the failed bank losing money, depositors at other banks sometimes went to their banks (in some haste) and, as a precaution, withdrew their deposits. When this happened, the entire system could quickly be drained of cash, and would fail. That would be disastrous for it would wipe out a large part of a country's money stock, and thus cause a severe recession. In those circumstances, the central bank acted as a lender of last resort. It lent cash, on the security of treasury bills and bills of exchange, to the banking system. The liquidity of the system was then restored and, as

[86]

experience of several such episodes has shown, so was confidence in the banking system.

The Bank of England acted as a lender of last resort in the way described several times in the 19th century. Walter Bagehot (in his book, *Lombard Street*, first published in 1873) is often credited with persuading the Bank to act in that way. But the Bank had so acted several times before his book appeared. What Bagehot did was to urge the Bank to make plain in advance that it stood ready to act as a lender of last resort whenever necessary. He argued that knowledge the Bank was willing to provide cash (in exchange for security) would itself help to prevent panic demands for cash emerging.

That description of the role of lender of last resort makes plain the role is narrow and precisely defined. If people flee with their deposits from one bank because they fear it to be unsound and about to fail, there is *no need* for lender-of-last-resort action if they flee not to cash but, as is more likely today, to another bank (as, for example, when Continental Illinois Bank in the USA was about to fail). In such circumstances, the system is not drained of cash; the cash is simply redistributed.

The 'last resort' role, and the analysis and evidence which explain and justify it, need never involve bailing out an insolvent bank. Not only is such action unnecessary; it is also undesirable, and usually for the central bank impossible. It is undesirable because if depositors know that banks will always be bailed out, they will go to the bank which, by taking the greatest risks can, at any rate for a time, pay the greatest returns to depositors and shareholders. For their part, banks will have few incentives to prudence, and will go for greatest returns almost regardless of risk. Bailing out banks would reward reckless behaviour.

Moreover, the central bank could seldom do it. Bailing out a bank requires an injection of new capital. Central banks do not have large balance sheets. They do not have the capital to bail out any but the tiniest of financial institutions. Hence it is the French taxpayer (via the French government), not the Banque de France, that is bailing out Credit Lyonnais.

To summarise, the lender of last resort is concerned with the stability of the monetary system, not that of individual banks. If for some reason a bank becomes insolvent, it should be allowed to fail.

[87]

Doing otherwise serves no good purpose. Bailing out Credit Lyonnais, as the French government is doing, is rewarding failure, *not* ensuring the stability of the French monetary system by acting as prudent lender of last resort.

June 1995

Central Banks Can Control Real Interest Rates

THE ABOVE IS A COMMON FALLACY. Evidence of its widespread acceptance is provided by a recent letter in the *Financial Times*, which ascribed the height of real interest rates in New Zealand to the behaviour of that country's central bank. And not only is the fallacy widespread, it is particularly dangerous because it contains a small trace of misleading truth. To see the fallacy it is useful to start with a definition.

The real interest rate is the interest rate after making allowance for change in the general level of prices. That real rate can be calculated in two quite different ways. The first way is to take the current nominal interest rate (the rate in money terms) and subtract from it the inflation rate over the *past* time period; usually the past year is the period chosen.

The second method is to take the current nominal interest rate and subtract from it the *expected* rate of inflation over the life (or, if it is shorter, the expected holding period) of the asset.

The two methods of course give roughly the same answer if the inflation rate is expected to be steady. Hence at moderate rates of inflation (say, below 5 per cent per annum), at which rates inflation does not change rapidly, the 'backward-looking' calculation is a good approximation to the 'forward-looking' one. But that is true only at such inflation rates; at higher rates it *may* be true, but is not inevitably so.

To see what, if anything central banks can do to real interest rates it is now useful to consider how interest rates are determined. The interest rate is a price. Like every other price, it moves around so as to equalise supply and demand: in this case, the supply of savings and the demand for funds to invest.

Savings and investment are both affected by real rates of interest – these are what tell savers how much their wealth will change by lending out their savings, and investors how much they are giving up by borrowing. Hence decisions to save and invest interact so as to determine the *real* rate of interest. An increase (for example) in expected inflation will then raise the nominal rate above the real rate by the amount of the inflation – because if it did not do so,

[89]

savers or investors or both would obtain different real returns from what they were satisfied with before.

Now with that analysis in mind it is possible to consider what influence central banks can have on real interest rates. One is obvious. They can make realised real rates turn out to be different from what was expected. This they can do by easing (or tightening) monetary policy in an unexpected way, thus making inflation over some period different from what it was expected to be over that period. This disappoints borrowers or lenders.

But that can *in itself* have no effect on the economy. For the borrowers or lenders are disappointed over decisions they have already taken. Whatever effect on the economy those decisions are going to have has either happened or, if there are long lags, is in train.

It is therefore clear that the power to affect the 'backward-looking' real interest rate gives the central bank no *direct* control over the economy. That does not, however, mean that it gives the central bank no *indirect* influence. It does, and the influence is always for the bad. Suppose the central bank is in the habit of producing unexpected changes in the inflation rate. Aside from any disruptive effects these have in other markets (and the evidence is the disruption is severe), it does great harm to the market for saving and investment. Savers would demand a large risk premium against accelerations of inflation, and investors a large risk premium against decelerations. The reluctance of savers to lend and investors to borrow would deter productive investment, and thus slow innovation and economic growth.

Can the central bank vary the 'forward-looking' real rate, that calculated as the money rate minus the expected rate of inflation? The answer is that it cannot. It can change expected inflation by changing its policies; and, whenever it does so, the nominal rate will change in line, so the central bank is impotent to affect this version of the real rate.

Now both the fallacy and the misleading grain of truth is clear. Central banks have no *sustained* influence over real rates of interest. They can for a very short time change real rates, by changing money rates over a time-period too short for inflation to change; this exercise, however, inevitably only harms the economy.

[90]

Central banks have no power for good over real interest rates, and no longer-lasting power over them at all.

March 1996

Part 6

Costs, Prices and Value

'Oil Companies Have Been Robbing the Public By Raising Prices When They Have Inventories Bought at Previous, Lower, Prices.'

THE ABOVE COMPLAINT against oil companies is an example – an example motivated by dramatic price movements – of a common and durable fallacy. The fallacy is to think that prices should be based on historic cost – what something used to cost, rather than an opportunity cost – what it is worth now.

The example of oil is a convenient one to use to analyse why prices should be determined by opportunity cost. Suppose oil companies hold stocks of oil, bought at a low price. The price of oil then rises. What if they sell all their stocks at the old price, and do not raise prices until new stocks have to be purchased?

Suppose first that oil prices rise but never fall. Every time there is a price rise, when oil companies have sold their stocks, they are unable to replace them without borrowing, running down assets or raising more capital.

If they behaved like this every time the price rose, what would happen? Their borrowing would rise without limit – of course, well before that, they would be unable to borrow and oil production would halt. Alternatively, they would run out of assets and oil production would halt. What of raising new capital? Does that help them out? Yet again the answer is 'no'. For who would invest in them if it were guaranteed that some of the investment would be lost whenever the price of raw materials went up?

In other words, under the assumption that oil prices can go up but not down, selling stocks at historic rather than opportunity cost guarantees that oil companies go out of business and that oil production ceases.

But of course oil prices both rise and fall. Does this affect the conclusion that stocks should be sold at opportunity cost? In this case, if companies always price at opportunity cost, they raise prices when raw material prices rise and lower them when they fall – thus making a 'windfall profit' when prices rise and a 'windfall loss' when they fall. In such a case, would pricing at historic cost not be quite satisfactory? For retail prices would still rise and fall, with a lag depending on how long it took for stocks to run down, and the viability of oil production would not be threatened. The answer is that even then historic cost pricing would be a dangerous error. Why? Because there is always the possibility that a change in oil price would not reverse, or that the trend was upwards. The contraction or extinction of the industry would again be threatened.

Pricing at opportunity cost has no harmful effects on the consumer in the short term, and avoids the threat of the industry collapsing. A similar analysis can be set out for falls in price – except that now, if pricing is at historic rather then opportunity cost, the industry expands without limit!

To conclude, then, pricing at opportunity cost produces efficient resource allocation. Pricing at historic cost can produce collapse of industries whose products people want and will pay for. Opportunity cost pricing is sensible and historic cost pricing foolish.

February 1991

Cutting Out the Middleman Brings Down Prices

SOMETIMES IN ADVERTISEMENTS consumers are exhorted to deal directly with the manufacturer, and by thus 'cutting out the middleman' save themselves money by buying the goods at a lower price. Middlemen are sometimes bracketed with 'racketeers' as people who raise prices to consumers – and often depress them to producers – as people, in fact, whose activities serve no good purpose. These advertisements and these criticisms (certainly so far as middlemen go) are misleading, for 'middlemen' serve a very useful purpose indeed.

There is an article, very famous to economists, called *On the Nature of the Firm.* In that article Ronald Coase (a Nobel Prize winner in Economics) asked why firms exist. Why, he asked, is each stage of production not carried out by independent contractors? The answer lies in the existence of transaction costs. Firms group together the parts of the production process which are best carried out by one organisation, rather then by a series of separate ones dealing with each other in the market-place.

This is why different industries are integrated – have production stages 'under one roof' – to different extents and also why firms in an industry can display different degrees of integration at different times. Different, and changing, technologies explain this observation; for they require different degrees of integration.

Realising this shows that the very definition of a middleman is not so straightforward as it seems. As technologies change, sometimes an activity – delivering the good, say – will be done by the firm, and sometimes a separate contractor. Surely it is ludicrous to describe the activity disparagingly, as parasitic, on some occasions, and as desirably productive on others, simply as a result of change in the ownership of the organisation which executes it.

'Middlemen' serve an economic purpose. They take the good from one place to another. They may buy large quantities and sell in smaller. They may hold inventories, so that the goods are continually available even though being produced only from time to time – in batches by the contractor or seasonally by Nature.

If the middleman is cut out, someone will have to do the job or jobs he did. And they will expect to be paid for doing so. Those who say, 'buy direct and cut out the middleman', are actually saying 'buy direct and use us as a middleman'. Unless they are willing to make losses, they must be paid for that activity. They are paid by higher prices or lower quality, offering smaller ranges, by insisting on buying in larger quantities, and no doubt by other means also. If there is not a 'middleman', all that has changed is that the task is done within the firm rather than by a separate organisation. 'Cutting out the middleman' effects no savings; for the middleman's work must still be done. Middlemen serve a useful function, and cannot be costlessly eliminated.

April 1992

What a Good Costs to Produce Determines its Worth

THE IDEA THAT if something is costly to produce then it is valuable pervades many aspects of life – even education, where now and again it is argued that someone deserves a good mark, or even a good degree, because he has 'worked hard'. But although all-pervasive, and indeed long-established, the belief is wrong.

When a person buys a good he is seeking to make himself (or the person for whom it is bought) as well off as possible, *given what he can afford to spend*. People thus look to see what provides the best value for their expenditure. How do we judge that?

What we look at is the satisfaction the good gives. In finding this out, people ask a whole range of questions. Is the good attractive? Is it reliable? Is it long-lasting? Or, perhaps, is the taste pleasing? Or, is it comfortable? The range can be added to considerably; which questions are appropriate depend of course on the nature of the good.

But every one of these questions is in essence a specific form of 'What will this good do for me?'. The questions are concerned with the *satisfaction* the consumption of the good provides. This satisfaction is (in general) independent of the effort and resources that have gone into producing the good. Consider the example of tomatoes. Suppose that at the same time in the year, tomatoes could be obtained from Scotland – by growing them in hot-houses which had been insulated and heated; or from, say, Morocco, where they grow in the open air with no attention except that needed to pick them. Would we pay more for the Scottish ones because they had been produced with more difficulty?

It is unlikely. Indeed, quite often there is no way the consumer can know – the goods are side by side, identical in all respects from the point of view of the satisfaction they give. If the information is absent it cannot affect the price!

There may be the occasional exception to this rule – people may value more something that is made by hand rather than by machine. But even here, what is usually valued is not being hand-made, but a *result* of that. Every example of the good will be slightly different from every other one – that is often an attraction.

Now, does this mean that costs of production do not matter at all? Of course it does not, but they do not matter for price. What they determine is whether the good continues to be supplied. Consider again the example of our valiant but misguided Scottish tomato grower. His costs of production will exceed the price at which he can sell his tomatoes. He will lose money, and leave the market, unless he both gets satisfaction from supplying the good and has some other source of income to allow continued subsidy of his tomato growing.

The point is a simple one. The conclusion that costs of production are irrelevant to price, and that price is determined by what consumers are willing to pay, follows directly from observing that people consume goods for the satisfaction they give. But although simple, it has widespread application, and ignoring it would lead to foolish decisions and to waste and misallocation of resources.

Take education. If someone is given a good degree because he has 'worked hard', think of the implication for a prospective employer. He will not be able to tell whether a prospective employee is a hard-working dunce or actually understands the subject of the degree. The qualification would give no information.

More generally, if goods were valued for the resources they use up rather than the satisfaction they give, resources would deliberately be used wastefully so as to increase the price of the output. This would diminish the supply of other goods that could be provided. It would be behaviour that created scarcity where there could have been abundance.

To conclude, the value of what has been used to produce a good – whether what has been used is effort or other types of scarce resources – is irrelevant to what the good is worth. Whether people will pay what it cost to produce is important, but important for determining if the good continues to be supplied. Goods are worth what people will pay for them, and that does *not* depend on their cost of production.

June 1994

Part 7
Labour Markets

'They're not Well Paid. They Should Get a Living Wage.'

WE OFTEN HEAR when a group of lower-paid workers goes on strike that they 'deserve more', that they 'need a living wage'. Although certainly well-meant, if followed that advice would end up making most people – particularly the low paid – worse off. It is useful to make the starting point of the discussion clear. Suppose that at the existing wage rate there are coming forward for work just the number of workers required, and that they work normal hours (that is, neither overtime nor short time on an average week) to meet demand for the product. These workers get together, and thinking that they are not paid a 'living wage', go on strike.

It is possible the employers could increase their wages; the employers might be monopolists, or they might be receiving a subsidy from the taxpayer to cover their costs. In any event, as a result of the increase in wages employers do not want to employ any fewer workers.

So the same number of workers is wanted, but higher wages are being paid. As this will lead to more workers applying, some – the *least able* – will be rejected. (It must be emphasised that this argument does not assume that people work only for money – what it assumes is that pay is one of the factors people are interested in.)

As a result of the wage increase some of the people who were previously in jobs are unemployed; and some of the people who have taken their place have come from other jobs where they are worth more, but are paid less because their employer is neither a monopolist nor subsidised to pay them more than the value they contribute to output.

This second effect, the diversion of more skilled workers, lowers the output of the economy. So we have more unemployment and less output as a result of 'paying a living wage'. This may seem a harsh conclusion. It is not. What it does is remind us that there are foolish ways as well as sensible ways to solve a problem.

In this case, the problem is that there are some jobs which are worth having done only at wages which society regards as too low – they provide too poor a standard of living. But paying more for these jobs makes things worse.

It is also worth looking at the case where the employer decides to pay the workers more, but cannot pass on this cost increase to either his customers or the general body of taxpayers.

The increased labour costs cannot be absorbed without increasing prices, for if they were other factors of production – raw materials and capital – could be paid less than they would earn elsewhere. The employer could not just cut back what he paid for raw materials; if he did, no-one would sell to him. So capital would end up earning less than it could elsewhere. This would lead to it being employed elsewhere. His only course is to charge more for his products, sell less, and employ fewer workers. Again unemployment rises.

What should, then, be done? What to do is to pay people money from general taxes. The people who receive this money can then go out and earn more without losing what they have already received.

If we simply decide to pay people more for their work without regard to what they produce, we will end up unable to pay them at all. Pay should be separate from social provisions – otherwise resources are wasted, and when that happens the poor are the first to suffer.

October 1989

'EC Gives Better Maternity Deal to UK Women'[1]

THE ABOVE QUOTATION, reporting an agreement on length of maternity leave and on maternity pay, was the headline above a story in which a substantial increase in these benefits was reported. The story also contained complaints that the agreement had been 'watered down'. To quote:

> 'Had the British government not watered [this] down, the whole community would be celebrating today. As it is, British women are just about the only ones who will benefit from the directive and, even with it, they remain at the bottom of the European heap when it comes to maternity rights.'

The fallacy involved is that workers are employed regardless of what they produce and what their labour costs.

If anyone were to assert boldly that employers did not care about their wage bills (a major part of their costs), they would of course just not be taken seriously. Firms which ignore their costs do not survive. And yet that is what the headline and, even more vigorously, the quotation, both imply.

The EC does not have an inexhaustible pot of gold from which it pays for the benefits it has imposed. It has no resources except those its member-governments raise by taxation. The private sector has to pay for these benefits.

Of course, these benefits are not being paid for by taxation. The costs of them will fall on firms which employ women. And that is only where they first impact. For what the legislation has done is raise the costs of employing women of child-bearing age relative to the costs of employing men, and women above child-bearing age.

So where will the costs fall? They will fall on young women who want to take jobs. These will find it harder to get jobs, and the jobs they will be offered will carry less pay than they would have before this legislation. Such women will thus be kept out of the workforce, or pushed into lower-paying activities. As a result of the legislation, women will be discriminated against on the

---

[1] *The Independent*, 21 October 1992.

perfectly good grounds that they have suddenly become more expensive.

Neither the EC nor any national government has resources to pay for the benefits they give. The cost falls on the private sector. In this case, the cost of better maternity pay and leave for pregnant women falls on other women. Despite the headline, the government is not, and never can be, Santa Claus.

February 1993

Social Dumping Is a Problem

SOME COUNTRIES IN THE EC, most recently France when Hoover moved its manufacturing from France to Britain, complain that other countries engage in 'social dumping'. By that they mean that having less restrictive labour legislation, and thus imposing lower costs on business, attracts jobs from one country to another. In an attempt to prevent this, the President of the EC Commission has tried to revive the 'social' part of the EC's plans, so as to prevent such competition.

There are two aspects to this issue. First, is 'social dumping' undesirable? And second, would M. Delors's scheme work? It is useful to take them in order, as the answer to the first bears on the second.

'Social dumping' does harm the countries which lose employment. They have a higher unemployment rate, and a lower level of national income. This happens simply because it is cheaper to do the work elsewhere. The other country (or countries) of course gain. Jobs are gained; output is gained; and income per head is higher.

The last is important. It happens because the size of the population does not go up, but the proportion of it which can work does. There is, in other words, clear gain for the country which gains the jobs.

What would happen if within some set of countries, 'social dumping' were prohibited? The effect would be to impoverish the whole area. Those in work *might* have better conditions – but recollect that output per head of population would be lower, so that countries as a whole would be worse off.

It might seem attractive to deal with the resulting unemployment by imposing tariff barriers – particularly against goods which had previously been produced domestically and were now imported. If these were high enough, they would re-direct production. But it would be high-cost production producing high-cost goods. The workforce might be increased – but wages would buy less.

The basic point, of course, is that we cannot get something for nothing. It may seem appealing to have a 'social charter' for workers. But that is not costless. The cost falls on the whole of society, including most notably those whom a desire to help workers drives out of work.

April 1993

'With Population Growth Continuing, It Will Be Harder and Harder to Find Jobs For Everyone.'

THERE WAS ONCE A FEAR that population growth would outstrip the growth of the world's food supply. The consequence was said to be that starvation would eventually constrain the size of the world's population. Thomas Malthus is often, not altogether fairly, identified with this 'Malthusian' doctrine. For the moment that fear has faded. Certainly one factor in that has been the growth in the EU of 'food mountains' – clear proof that if you pay enough, more will be produced.

A modern variant of this fear is that the supply of jobs is limited, and will inevitably be outstripped by the number of those wanting to find work. Occasionally governments in recent years have acted in part on the prompting of these fears. The French government, for example, has given incentives to firms to reduce hours worked per worker so as to increase numbers of workers employed. (The immediate cause of their action may well have been France's persistently high unemployment rate; but the notion of a permanent 'jobs shortage' certainly helped.)

Notice first that there is some measure of inconsistency between the so-called 'Malthusian' fear and the fear of a job shortage. The former implies that there are no limits to what people will consume. The latter implies that there are limits.

Showing that the belief in a permanent jobs shortage is fallacious is best done in two stages.

First, note what happens when any individual gets richer. In all but a tiny minority of ascetics, that individual consumes more. Not necessarily more of the same thing, although more pairs of shoes or more shirts, for example, may well be bought. What happens as an individual gets richer is that a bigger range of goods and services is consumed. Man has an infinite capacity for discovery, and this capacity is not limited to the discovery of new medicines. As the centuries have passed people have consumed more varieties of clothes, carpets, foods, books, and entertainments. The habit of going to theatres and concerts developed. The cinema was invented, the television, the record player, and so forth. The steam

[109]

engine and the motor car replaced the horse as a means of transport – although (a good illustration of a point made below) the horse continued to be used in leisure activities.

The time may yet come when mankind is sated with consumption – but it has not come yet, and shows no signs of doing so. On those grounds alone, there is no reason for believing that there will be no jobs for a growing population. That population will, on the evidence so far available, find work producing increasing varieties of goods to be consumed.

But the argument that there is no danger of a long-run shortage of jobs does not end there. Suppose people do start to consume a smaller fraction of income. This means inevitably, as a matter of arithmetic, that a larger fraction of it is saved. Rising savings will tend to lower rates of interest and, in turn, to encourage investment. If capital is used increasingly relative to labour in the production of goods, the earnings of labour will be pulled up. This will have two effects – living standards will rise and, a consequence of that, working hours will fall. Leisure is something people like to consume. They will consume more of it, and engage increasingly in time-consuming leisure activities. Note, as mentioned above, the survival of the horse for use in leisure activities, and the growth in the popularity of golf, a prodigiously time-consuming sport.

To summarise so far then, a rising population will not encounter a fixed number of jobs. *First*, because this rising population will itself want to consume. *Second*, because technical progress (which shows no signs of slowing) will lead to the production of an ever-expanding range of consumer goods. And *third*, because as the earnings of labour rise, people will wish to consume more leisure. All these have occurred over the past centuries. (Not necessarily at a steady rate, of course; working hours, for example, have floated up and down, but about a falling trend.) The forces which have ensured that jobs have been available in the past for an ever-expanding population are all rooted in mankind's desires to consume and to enjoy leisure. So long as these fundamental human motives remain jobs will be created.

Of course this does not mean that there will never be an unemployment problem. There can be temporary fluctuations in unemployment, related to the business cycle. And unemployment can be created by well-intended but ill-designed social legislation.